David's New Bike

A Book about Being Active

by Kerry Dinmont

Published by The Child's World®
1980 Lookout Drive • Mankato, MN 56003-1705
800-599-READ • www.childsworld.com

Photographs ©: Monkey Business Images/iStockphoto, cover, 1, 3, 4, 5,
13; Shutterstock Images, 8, 15, 16; Africa Studio/Shutterstock Images, 10–11;
Monkey Business Images/Shutterstock Images, 18–19, 20

ISBN 9781503820234
LCCN 2016960945

Printed in the United States of America
PA02340

Today, David got a new bike!

How does biking help
keep him **active**?

Biking gets David up and moving. It keeps him healthy.

8

Biking works David's heart and lungs. This keeps his body strong.

Exercise helps David **relax**. He sleeps better at night.

David wears a helmet.
A helmet protects his
head.

David stops at stop signs. He watches for cars.

David rides on a path.
He races to the park.
He bikes fast!

Staying active
makes David's
body strong.

How were you active today?

Glossary

active (AK-tiv) Being active means doing something that involves moving around. Biking is a way to be active.

relax (ree-LAX) To relax is to not be tense or nervous. Activity helps you relax.

Extended Learning Activities

1. After reading this book, why do you think you should be active?

2. Think of a time you biked. Where were you? How did you stay safe?

3. What sort of rules do people who ride bikes have to follow?

To Learn More

Books

Heos, Bridget. *Be Safe on Your Bike.*
Mankato, MN: Amicus, 2015.

Rockwell, Lizzy. *The Busy Body Book: A Kid's Guide to Fitness*. New York, NY: Crown Publishers, 2008.

Web Sites

Visit our Web site for links about being active:
childsworld.com/links

Note to Parents, Teachers, and Librarians: We routinely verify our Web links to make sure they are safe and active sites. So encourage your readers to check them out!

About the Author

Kerry Dinmont is a children's book author who enjoys art and nature. She lives in Montana with her two Norwegian elkhounds.